Playful Relationship Advice for Understanding Your Man

Michael Coogan & William Burton

Know Your Pig!™
Playful Relationship Advice for Understanding Your Man(Pig)

ISBN: 0-9788176-1-3
978-0-9788176-1-9

Published and Distributed by;

Global Focus
2710 Thomes Ave., Suite 370
Cheyenne, WY 82001

Order Information
To order more copies of this book or to receive a complete
Catalog of other products by Michael Coogan and William Burton
contact us at *info@knowyourPig.com*

Acknowledgements

"When you drink the water,
think of those who dug the well"
~ Chinese Proverb

MANY THANKS TO THE litter of Pigs, women and friends that contributed to this book. Some are shy and have chosen not to be publicly acknowledged. They know who they are (and so do we) and we thank them for their open insights and contributions.

Special thanks to the following friends and family; Christy C, Erin C, Vicki F, Wendy B, Tina G, Jessica K, Vanessa G, Peg Q, Leslie T, Rebecca D, Lucy O, Susan S, Nellika R, Myra P, Diane B, Merillee S, AJS; The Man Who Dug the Well, The Many Men and Teams of NoM, Phillipe L, Bob W, James C, Bill B, Nicolas S, Haroun S, Luke D, Andy W, Paul A, Charles L, Greg A, Rich R, Bill P, Steve C and Ron P.

Bill Friend

Bill is a friend of both authors and created our business card logos as a gift for the project. He's a natural graphic artist and ingenious at crafting designs from a simple conversation.

Cajun Pepper

Cajun Pepper Studio is about personality! Their work exemplifies their passion for character-driven storytelling. Their studio produces everything from cutting-edge 3D graphics and animation to stunning effects for the Web, HDTV, and film. Cajun Pepper goes above and beyond to "put a little pep in your step!" *www.cajunpepper.com*

Diane Darling

Diane Darling is a freelance writer, editor and event producer with a background in magazine publication, book editing and ghostwriting. She's completing her first novel — a retelling of the Persephone/Hades myth from ancient Greece. She lives in northern California with her friends and a small parrot.

Dedication

This book is dedicated to women around the world who see the humorous side of trying to understand the men in their lives.

Table of Contents

Introduction — Why We Wrote This Book ix
Our Expert Credentials xi
The Character Types xii
Men are Pigs!!! 1
What Type of Pig Do You Have? 5
The Six States 9
Tips and Tricks 29
Communication 41
The Matrix 59
The Pig Types 63
Putting it all together 71
Suggested Reading List 79

Introduction — Why We Wrote This Book

> *"There is much more truth in a metaphor than in a fact."*
> ~ Norman Mailer

MEN ARE PIGS!...... How many times have women thought, heard, said, emailed or screamed that sentence out of anger or frustration? Once? Twice? A hundred times? A gazillion?

We believe that men and women would get along better if we only understood each other better. As males, we understand each other very well. We know then — and are willing to confess that — while we usually respond to the "Men are Pigs!" statement by protesting, "I am not!" — deep down we want to scream, "Yes, yes, I am a Pig *and damn proud of it!*"

But before we get there — a simple caveat: I need you ladies to understand what *Type* of Pig I am and what *State* I am in before I let you into my world.

Given the above, it made sense to us and our other Pig acquaintances that a tongue in cheek handbook was absolutely necessary to help the females in our lives to *Know and Understand Your Pig.*

This book is a result of many mens gatherings — formal and informal, with new and old friends. Together we have shared, discussed, complained, oinked and snorted, all in the hopes that our significant others (usually female) understood us better. We wrote the book on behalf of anyone who has ever thought about a new approach or a simple system for understanding, maintaining, experiencing, communicating and getting along with us Pigs.

As you read through the book, look between the larger concepts for hints and tips you might find useful and think of them as kernels of corny wisdom.

Our Expert Credentials

This is the place where most authors present their qualifications, training and general suitability for pontificating on their topics. They lay out their credentials, such as PhD in psychology, relationship therapist, author of a dozen other books on the subject, and so forth. We can only claim that we are lifelong Pigs and have had a lot of experiences, both individually and together, as Pigs. Everyone else involved in this project is either a Pig or has grown up with, worked with, dated, or married one (or more). From the "research" we've gathered in our relationships, cocktail parties, and working lives, we know we are fully qualified to speak for and about normal healthy Pigs. This book is our effort to do so with light hearts and pointed humor.

The Character Types

There are multiple types of personality tests on the market that can tell you a lot about a person including the way they think, act and view the world. If you search the Web you'll find many sites that allow you to examine yourself and others. Some tests are free while others charge for this service (if you see it as such!). If you're looking to try your hand at self-analysis, there are many online tests found as easily as a quick search on Google™.

Understanding and determining a person's character takes time, effort, and is a task that should always be taken with careful consideration. We've chosen to interpret a popular Enneagram test at a very high level for the character types we define in this book. This method, in our opinion, is a well rounded and grounded test.

Another caveat: the advice and observations we offer are truly our own, as is each mistake and act of folly, and should in no way be attributed to or blamed on anyone other than ourselves. Same goes for strokes of genius.

1

Men Are Pigs!!!

> *"Everything should be made as simple as possible — but not simpler!"*
> ~ Albert Einstein

LADIES, LET'S TALK ABOUT PIGS. Not the smelly, foul tempered four legged variety. I'm talking about the smelly, foul tempered, messy and ill mannered two legged ones that you live with, work with and have most assuredly dated. The ones that wallow in filth and call it "football." Who drink beer and eat pizza thinking they have had a balanced meal because they got the veggie topping and a lite beer.

And just when it seems like you finally get a man home and really get to know him — no matter whether he wears a Brooks Brothers™ suit, a cowboy hat or overalls — there is always a little pink Pig underneath. Search in any man's closet and you'll find a worn out sweatshirt, faded blue jeans, and a stained, hole-filled college drinking team t-shirt. When you do, you'll know, as you might have suspected from the beginning, you are in the presence of a real Pig.

Let's be fair, not all men are Pigs. The problem really lies with the men who *aren't* Pigs — while they are often cute, cuddly and kind to begin with, they may not have the strength of character you really need — and want — in a long term partner.

As Pigs ourselves, we ask you — are you just going to sit back and accept the cruel reality that Men are Pigs? To listen to what your mother, sisters, girlfriends and Tim Allen have been saying for years? The answer is YES, dear girl, YES!

We've all been through the Pig selection process (aka: the dating game) right? You chose your Pig based on instinct, took him home, and sooner or later discovered that you had the wrong Pig. You tried to train him, but that just made him ill-tempered and even more ornery. You were forced to dump your Pig back on the market and head back into the pen (dating scene) looking for a new one. This repetitive pattern meant you usually ended up with someone else's rejected Pig — a guy who looked good at first but ended up having the same old Pig issues as before. In fact, he might be even worse than the one you just got rid of! This cycle can continue for years as you search for that special Pig to spend your life with.

TIP: *Just remember, no matter how "cute" that new guy across the room looks, or how funny and nice he may be, somewhere there is a woman who is tired of putting up with his Pigness.*

A bleak forecast to be sure. So is there any hope? Again, YES, dear girl, YES! From this point on you are entering the world of the Pig — a world where you'll learn how their simple little minds work, the secret ways of the Pig, and the tactics needed to train and manage him like a real professional. By following a few simple steps, you'll be rewarded with a well-behaved partner who is successfully house-broken but hasn't lost that fun-loving Piggy joie de vivre.

If all men are Pigs — and the best ones are — then you need to learn the way of the Pig: to train, manage and care for your own special little oinker. This book is intended to help all women who find themselves standing on the brink of a relationship and discovering... "Oh my God, they're all Pigs!"

What you should have learned in this chapter

- Men are Pigs.
- Women have to spend time with Pigs, one way or another. There is no way to avoid this.
- With the help of this book, it's possible to coexist with Pigs in an intelligent, considerate way.

2

What Type of Pig Do You Have?

"All women become like their mothers. That is their tragedy. No man does. That's his."
~ Oscar Wilde

"I married beneath me, every woman does."
~ Lady Astor

IF THERE IS ONE CONSISTENT error women make when trying to understand their Pig it's that they overestimate their Pig's capabilities. When it comes to relationships and communication, Pigs are far less skilled than you might imagine. This places the responsibility for training your Pig solely on you because in this specific area, women are far superior. It's not that Pigs are stupid or lack intelligence; it's just that the complexities and nuances of communication and relationship are lost on a brain optimized to take advantage of a hydromatic 5-speed transmission and the proper application of the designated hitter rule. "What?" you ask? To help understand this challenging element of Pig management we've spared no expense in conducting exhaustive field research and scientific analysis of Pig behavior, swinish attitudes, motivations, emotional reactions, defense mechanisms, Piggy interests and porkish potential. Our research has concluded there are nine basic Pig Types, each with specific characteristics and attitudes that, when understood, can assist you in the proper selection and management of the right Pig for you.

Understanding your Pig's dominant Type is essential in understanding your Pig's motivation and priorities. In turn, this becomes the basis for a proper training regimen. Once you have identified your Pig's Type, a successful relationship becomes exponentially more possible as you tailor your own speech (speaking their language) and behavior (operant conditioning) to elicit the desired response from your Pig.

Communication is a critical component of successful Pig management. We'll cover this in more detail in a later chapter, but be assured that understanding the Pig Types will allow you to open clear communication channels and prepare you to deal effectively with conflicts, ineffective work habits, unacceptable behaviors and office politics. In essence, learning and understanding the nine basic Pig Types is fundamental to making your life with a Pig worth living.

Let's not forget that your personal style is also a major factor in how successful you are at dealing with each type of Pig. Not all Pigs are compatible with your particular style and the key is knowing which Pig Type is best suited for your style.

We highly recommend that you begin to look for

you'll begin to recognize each Type and understand their specific behaviors and reactions.

It's important to understand that these Pig Types have a neutral value. That is, one Type is not "better" or "worse" than another. Your Pig preference is a matter of taste and your own personality type and history. One Pig Type that is repugnant to you may be the most desirable boar in the pen to your best friend. In different settings and for different purposes, qualities of different Pig Types are more desirable, useful, or repulsive. It's also important to note that these Pig Types apply to Pigs from pens around the world. And when a Pig is born, their dominant Pig Type is set for life. Sorry ladies — you may as well give up changing your Pigs Type. Trying to change your Pigs fundamental type or characteristics is like trying to teach a real pig to sing. It is futile and REALLY annoys the pig! A Pig can, however, exhibit a wide range of behaviors within his Type, according to his level of development. We will get into the detailed analysis of the nine Types later, but let's take a brief overview:

The Nine Primary Pig Types

Type One: The Excellence Pig
Type Two: The Charitable Pig
Type Three: The Acrobat Pig
Type Four: The Sentimental Pig
Type Five: The Watcher Pig
Type Six: The Unbeliever Pig
Type Seven: The Gourmet Pig
Type Eight: The Guard Pig

What you should have learned in this chapter

- Pigs are way simpler than you thought.
- Understanding and responding to your Pig's personality Type makes everything easier.
- There are only nine Pig Types.
- Attempting to change a Pigs Type is futile.

3

The Six States

> *"I know that you believe that you understood what you think I said, but I am not sure you realize that what you heard is not what I meant."*
> ~ Robert McCloskey, State Department spokesman

As you'll hear several times in this book, Pigs are simple. We're not saying they're stupid, it's just that their brains, body chemistry and emotions operate in a much simpler way than those of women. Nowhere is this more observable than when it comes to emotional states. While women can define hundreds of emotional states, each with its own subtleties, men have just six primary emotional states. For men more evolved on the emotional axis there may be a few more, but for most men six — and only six — emotional states drive the majority of their actions, behaviors and most importantly their interactions with you.

This can be observed when you ask a man how he's feeling (not a recommended question once you understand your Pig). You'll find that he doesn't immediately understand or relate to the question. His most frequent response is a blank stare and a mumbled "huh?" Next, you find that he stumbles for even a hint of what might be going on. This usually involves a near seizure-like expression followed by a blank stare reminiscent of a deer caught in the headlights of an SUV on a country road late at night. At this point, even if he can actually identify what feeling he may have, he then has to try and associate a word with that emotion or feeling. This requires the left and right sides of the brain to communicate; however, since that particular pathway is often jammed with priority communication (such as whether lite beer is really less filling), the result is often a quick "nothing." He isn't trying to deceive, mislead or cover up what he's feeling — it's just that all too often what he really is feeling is, well, "nothing."

A word about evolution here (yes we proclaim to be experts in this area too — we are Pigs afterall!). Throughout history men have been hunters. As such, they were often faced with scary and dangerous circumstances. If a man actually stopped to figure out what he was feeling in the midst of pouncing on a woolly mammoth with nothing but a wooden club he would have wet himself, crawled under the nearest rock and waited for the invention of the Big Mac®. Evolution cut the circuits to his emotional awareness so that he would actually do crazy things like slay dragons, drive stock cars and capture that little black spider crawling on the bedroom ceiling.

As a result, we are left with an emotionally inert descendant of the cave man who is not only unaware of his feelings but also virtually incapable of describing them — no matter how many PhDs in Nuclear Physics or Celestial Mechanics he has. Again, this is not a result of stupidity or lack of education, it's a lack of the fundamental wiring necessary to do anything but fight, flight or freeze.

Let's explore these six States in order to gain an understanding of what drives your Pigs' behavior and reactions. Actually — wait — we've to stop for a minute here — I can hear you saying right now..."it can't be this simple! Men have to be more complex than this!?" Trust us, they aren't. There really are six and only six primary States. Pigs are simple...repeat after me, PIGS ARE SIMPLE.

TIP: *Your Pig's State at any given time probably has no more to do with you than the brand of beer he prefers*

And one more thing — *it's not your fault!* Whatever State your Pig is in at any time is probably not your fault. Women, whether by conditioning or evolutionary design, seem to want to feel responsible for a Pig's state of mind. This is natural since in most couple relationships the woman takes on the role of caregiver, sensitive to the moods and feelings of those around her. Frequently a woman will assume that she must be the reason her Pig is upset, that it's her fault in some way. This is rarely the case, however, and we suggest practicing letting go of any ownership of your Pig's emotional State.

So what are these six States? We're glad you asked...

Happy
Hungry
Hurried
Horny
Angry
Tired

From a Pig's perspective, virtually every feeling, including those micro-emotions only women understand, falls into one of these six primary States.

And we're not just talking about your Pig here, but also the ones you work with, the ones at the grocery store, the ones that fix your car, and the ones you meet at parties. All are Pigs. All possess just six emotional States.

Knowing what State your Pig is in can help you tremendously with your relationship and communication, and suggests a number of interesting behavioral strategies. A lot of dreary issues can easily be avoided if you know the State of your Pig and how to respond to it, use it and change it. By categorizing any Pig situation based on these six States you are able to observe the behavior of your Pig and respond in ways that result in a happy Piggy and a happy you.

But first a word of caution: with a mere six States, Pigs are typically more intense than their women counterparts who are capable of experiencing a multitude of emotional States. Pigs are rarely "a little hungry" — when they get hungry they need to be fed. Period. When Pigs get angry it tends to be very intense but doesn't usually last long. Recognize this in men and you'll be much more equipped to keep your cool when your Pig devours an entire bag of chips before dinner.

The State your Pig is in will determine, to a formidable degree, how he reacts to your needs, requests or communication. For example, if he's in a Hurried State, he's unlikely to listen to anything you say, let alone admit into his consciousness that you want to talk about something on a deeper level. If you persist in your effort to communicate when he's Hurried, you'll likely end up with a frustrated or maybe even Angry Pig. On the other hand, if you stay out of the way and let your Pig work his way out of Hurried and into Happy he'll be much more willing to engage in communication or at least attempt to listen to what you have to say.

Delving deeper, if a Pig is hungry, he's definitely going to be on the hunt for food to eat now. Anyone or anything that comes between him and getting food will be seen as an obstruction to overcome or avoided completely. This is not a good time to try and get his attention about an important matter. Feed him however, (many good Pig managers carry Piggy Treats in their purses) and you'll have a happy Pig who you can approach with comfort and ease.

Keep it simple when tailoring how you interact with your Pig's state of mind — and be realistic about the results you want from him. Most women try and make this way too complicated. Identify the State he's in, what need he has from you (if any) at that moment, and then wait for his State to modify to one that is conducive to your purpose. Generally, if a Pig is in a particular State, he has to complete that State before moving into another one.

You'll sometimes experience Pigs in multiple States, though one is typically dominant over the others. Despite this perceived complexity of emotions, Pigs in more than one State are still much simpler than women believe.

Start observing Pigs every time you encounter them and ask yourself, "What State is he in right now?" You'll be surprised how easy it is to do this once you start to practice. It's pretty much what you see is what you get so don't try and make it complicated.

Let's take a closer look at each of the six States.

Happy

A Happy Pig is light-hearted, smiley, engaging with people (including you), and kind to small animals. Happy is often a result of some good news, a positive work experience, a sporting event, a recent sexual encounter or the perfect BBQ grilling experience. The Pig has achieved or exceeded his own expectations, whether it was a task laid out for him or one he chose for himself. In short, Happy is anything that has inflated his ego.

When your Pig is Happy, many more things are possible because it enhances all other States when they occur together. For example, Happy is a good State when going out to dinner (just don't let him get too hungry — Hungry trumps Happy), making love (as compared to just having sex), flying kites, and buying CDs. Please don't waste Happy on cleaning out the garage or checking email. Get in the game and make the most of it!

Hungry

Hungry is an important State to watch out for, and fortunately it's also a slam dunk. A Hungry Pig is only focused on getting and eating food. Pigs are designed to graze and need to be fed regularly throughout the day. Too much time between belly grumbling and eating can easily throw a Pig into an Angry State,. A Hungry Pig will stay focused on getting food until he has it in his belly (oh, and hopefully a beer in hand).

It's important to note that Hungry can often look like anger or impatience. If your Pig is unpleasant and hasn't eaten lately, start by feeding him. This will often resolve what appears to be a much more complex issue or State. A simple treat given to "hold him over" will often make life with a Hungry Pig bearable until you can find a bigger portion of food to satisfy him. For this reason, a knowledgeable and prepared Pig manager will often carry a selection of snacks in a convenient location like her purse or glove box. These Piggy Treats can often save embarrassing and upsetting conflicts with a Hungry Pig.

It's useful to note that a Pig's ability to hear is inversely proportional to his hunger — the hungrier a Pig gets, the less he hears and understands. It's like a large church bell ringing louder and louder in his head the longer he goes without food. The bell drowns everything out unless it has a direct connection with sourcing food.

Hungry should be checked for regularly, but asking "Are you hungry" is doing more harm than good because he's always hungry. Try quantifying his level of hunger and ask, "How hungry are you?" or "How soon do you want to eat?" then do the math. A Pig's hunger ranges from "no, not hungry," meaning, "I'm not hungry now but will be soon," to "I'm hungry," meaning "I need to eat soon or that damn bell is going to get louder and louder and I'm going to be a real pain in the ass until I get food!"

Hurried

A Hurried Pig is like a train barreling down the tracks — it's best not to get in the way. Your Pig is focused on getting down the track as directly as possible to accomplish his tasks and objectives. If you absolutely must engage a Hurried Pig, be direct, brief and to the point. Instead of standing on the tracks, step to the side and send a brief message to the conductor as he goes by. Let your Pig know you understand his State, that you have a request, and that you look forward to talking to him when he's in a State to hear you.

TIP: *The best Pig communications are done in 25 words or less. Short, sweet, direct and to the point.*

One rule of thumb for a Hurried Pig communication: make it 25 words or less. Leave off any unnecessary preamble ("I was talking to Mary about the party next week…"), any unnecessary information ("…her sister will be in town, you know the one that had the gall bladder surgery last year…"), or any reference to emotional conflict ("…I'm not sure how I feel about those new drapes she bought since I'm not that fond of sea foam green…") — get to the facts. Just the facts. "I need you to bring the charcoal grill to Mary's party next week." That's it, 25 words or less and you'll likely get a positive response from your Hurried Pig. If your communication comes across as rude, then you are probably about right for the Hurried Pig. We should say that even after the simplified version, there is only a 25% chance that he'll remember to do what you asked him to do. The fall back plan in this case means creating a Honey-Do-List, but we'll cover that topic later on.

Depending on his Pig Type, if you handle the Hurried Pig well, he might even blow the whistle for you as he goes by, or toss you a kiss or a "thanks for understanding." It can happen, trust us. Most Pigs return to their ladies in a much more relaxed State if they know they didn't run her over along the way.

Horny

Some women will say that Pigs only have one State: Horny. This is simply not true, though it's consistently in the top three — at least for the first half of a healthy Pig's life.

> **TIP:** *It has been wisely said that God gave men a brain and a penis but only enough blood to operate one at a time.*

When a Pig is Horny, he uses all his charm, looks and wiles to get laid. He's Horny and he wants his curly tail pulled! Of course, the relationship you have with your particular Pig will determine how you deal with him. A Pig can be Horny even though you are not the legitimate object of his lust.

Horniness predisposes a Pig to say "yes" to almost any request. As women, you already know this. And Pigs are aware that women know this. So please be kind.

Remember, we aren't all that aware in the first place — and in some kind of cosmic joke from God, he gave us a brain and a penis but only enough blood to operate one at a time. I reiterate — please be kind!

A Horny Pig is the easiest Pig to manage. Due to loss of blood flow to the brain, if you have a Horny Pig you have a stupid Pig. It will obey your every command and follow you where ever you lead especially if he has concluded there might be sex in his short-term furture. Too little Horny (too much sex) and they get sleepy and lazy. Too Horny, and they just get stupid beyond belief. It's also worth noting that a Horny Pig often suffers from a case of total memory loss following sex *(post coital amnesia)*. He'll likely remember almost nothing he said or agreed to the night before. Ya, we're all Pigs!

Angry

Watch out! An Angry Pig is worse than a Hurried Pig — just don't assume it's about you. We do not condone Pigs taking their anger out with physical, verbal or mental abuse on women. That's what gladiatorial sports like football, hockey and freeway driving are for.

TIP: *If an Angry Pig tells you to "get out his face" or "leave me alone" you should take this seriously and remove yourself from his presence at once. No further constructive interaction is possible or should occur until the Pig has modified his State.*

Angry is a State like any other but since we Pigs have so few States, it can be very intense. Angry isn't the time to try and snuggle in close. And it's certainly not the time to try and communicate with your Pig. But maybe the worst offence in this case is telling an Angry Pig, "Don't be angry." If he had the emotional capacity, he would say that this invalidates him and makes him feel that he's wrong to feel what he's feeling. Instead, what he hears from you is "Hey, go ahead and get really pissed off 'cause you're not pissed off enough"!!! It just makes him angrier and he'll end up distancing himself from you.

We recommend learning from your Pig (another time — not when he's angry) what he thinks and feels, and his idea of what the fair and helpful rules of engagement are when he's angry. Pigs all have ways they prefer to be dealt with when they're angry. Learn your Pig's special tricks and make sure you don't get sucked in — just remember, it's probably not about you anyway. There is a reason they say "you always hurt the ones you love": anger is a vortex that will suck in everything close to the Angry Pig unless you understand how you can help without becoming part of the problem. Successfully being with an Angry Pig can often look like standing in the eye of a tornado while the houses, cars and cows fly all around you. Stay centered in the eye and wait for the storm to pass — it most surely will.

TIP: *When confronted by an Angry Pig it is probably not about you. Get to the eye of the storm, stay centered and watch for flying debris.*

Tired

Yaaaawwwnnnnnnn!!!! Ahhhhh.. That feels better...

A Tired Pig has the opposite reaction to that of a Hungry Pig. Instead of a bell ringing in his ears, it's like someone has filled them with cotton. A Tired Pig operates poorly and gets disoriented easily. His brains turn to Jell-O® and thought processes revert to simple States (like Hungry and Horny). Occasionally Tired will move to Angry, but usually it takes too much energy to be angry, compared to just sinking down into a pillow...just for a few minutes...zzzzz....

> **TIP:** *Anything a Pig says within 15 minutes of falling asleep is inadmissible in any future discussion or argument.*

Your Tired Pig is apt to make decisions for decision's sake, not based on logical reasoning or good advice. Be careful to ensure your Pig is not

Tired when you bring up important things like marriage or your visiting mother. A Pig will answer in the affirmative when he's trying to get out of the conversation and go to sleep. Responses elicited from a Pig who is Tired or actually sleeping do not count later when he awakens *(post nocturnal amnesia)*. Did I mention we are all Pigs?!

What you should have learned in this chapter

- Whatever your Pig's State, it's simpler than you think and it's probably not about you.
- Six States (Happy, Horny, Hurried, Angry, Hungry, Tired) account for 90% of a Pig's emotional life.
- These States tend to be intense.
- In the stressed States of Angry, Hungry, Hurried, and Tired put all important communications on hold or make them simple and succinct so that you can both come back to it when he's Happy or Horny.
- In short :

  – If he's Angry, let him blow.

  – If he's Hungry, let him eat.

  – If he's Hurried, let him go.

  – If he's Tired, let him rest.

  – If he's Happy, go for it.

  – If he's Horny, be kind.

4

Tips and Tricks

"Always carry a litterbag in your car. It doesn't take up too much space, and when it gets full, you can throw it out the window!"
~ Steve Martin

HERE WE OFFER SOME useful advice about how to deal with your Pig so that you both win. Win? Who said anything about win or lose? In case you didn't already know, it's *always* about win or lose for Pigs. That's how our brains are wired. We hate ties (yes, both kinds) which is why in most of our sports we go to great lengths to make sure the game ends with one winner and one loser. Let a Pig win or at least think he has won and you'll have a Happy Pig.

The following kernels of wisdom may be small, but if followed consistently you'll have a happy, satisfied, contented Pig who eagerly awaits your next desire.

Lists

Pigs are task orientated. They love to do stuff, especially if it involves old clothes, explosives, beer, winning or buying a new tool. For both of you to be fulfilled by his work, he needs written lists that are easy to use and understand. By this we mean lists that are short, doable and written on a piece of paper that he can put in his pocket.

TIP: *If you want your Pig to focus on three or more items, the list MUST be written.*

When creating lists, there are some rules:

After you've indicated what you want him to do, you can tell your Pig *how* to do it or *when* to do it, but not both — that just frustrates him.

Leave a little creative flexibility and he'll get more done in the long run.

Include the ideal timeframe for each task to be completed, but don't tell him how to go about it!

TIP: *Your Pig will probably not complete any task in the same way you might. Focus on the result, not the process.*

A word of warning here: Make sure that you are very specific about what outcome you are expecting. "Paint the bedroom "leaves WAY too much open for Pig interpretation. "Paint the bedroom in two coats of Sherman-Williams® Desert Sunset (#1074)" is better. Otherwise you'll likely have one bedroom the color of Rusty Wallace's racing suit or The Dallas Cowboys Cheerleaders® skirts.

Do not keep adding to the list once the Pig has started checking things off. If it doesn't make it on the list before you give it to him, start a new list for later. Don't frustrate your Pig by moving his reward farther away because you forgot something.

A Honey-Do list should never be more than about five items long. More than that will simply overwhelm the Pig and you'll likely see no action.

Preferred rewards range from a simple thank you, to dinner, unstructured time, attention to his projects, food, football and, of course, sex.

Make sure you deliver on the reward within a short time of his completing the task list. Non-delivery can frustrate and piss off your Pig, and he'll feel you've let him down on your end of the bargain.

TIP: Big Hint: *Reward your Pig when he's completed his list. If you really want to motivate him, put his reward at the bottom of the list so he's motivated to complete it.*

Lists fall into three categories: Shopping, Maintenance or Honey-do.

Shopping

If you send your Piggy to a store to pick up some things and don't provide him with a list, he'll come back with 95 things and not one of them will be what you wanted. Pigs are simple, smart and creative creatures, but anything more then three items requires a list. Items on a grocery lists may seem obvious but require key descriptors such as brand, size, type and quantity. Make a list that is easy to use and reward based. He'll find it informative, instructional and it will even make shopping a bit like a treasure hunt, something Pigs consider fun.

Maintenance

Vehicle maintenance is probably one of the few reasons Pigs are worth tolerating and it's a task that can be scheduled way in advance and agreed upon so as not to disrupt your Pig's sports schedule, hammock time, pleasure trip or business function. This can also be true of pool and hot tub maintenance, taking the garbage bins to the curb, and other recurring tasks. Weekly and monthly chores can be noted on a calendar that is hung where it's easy for him to see. Who are we kidding — no Pig is going to check his chore calendar. Face it ladies, you are going to have to remind him...sorry!

Honey-do

Honey-do lists are for things that need doing sporadically, like cleaning gutters, plumbing, or putting up a clothesline. Don't clutter your honey-do list with things your Piggy will do on his own anyway like getting the barbecue ready or putting up the hammock. Prioritize the tasks; keep each list doable, and reward, reward, reward.

Accepting Your Pig's Friends

Pigs need other Pigs. You can't be everything to him (sorry), and you really don't want to engage in most "important" Pig rituals, such as watching back-to-back football games, drinking beer and talking about sports, going out after work to a tavern full of working Pigs, fishing, or working on car engines.

Women tend to bond with others more naturally than men. Evolutionary survival, cultural conditioning and a need for intimacy (with and without sex) all predispose women to relate more readily than Pigs. This is a natural trait of most Pig Types and should not be considered a flaw.

Pigs bond when they're little, but when separated from their littermates they become independent and self-sufficient. As they get older, Pigs take longer to make new, real friends. It's important to encourage and support your Pig and a few of his close friends. This takes the burden off you and allows your Pig to get the special support that only a fellow Pig can give.

Pig Trips

Despite their generally independent and competitive nature, Pigs need to get together in groups from time to time. Once or twice a year encourage your Pig to get together with his Pig friends for a weekend. Whether a fishing trip, hunting retreat or just a boys weekend, your Pig will return from these weekends with a new respect for his home, his woman and his family.

Hint: Big points if you help your Pig get ready for the trip, assuring him that he does not need to check in with you while he's away unless it's an emergency.

If you have concerns about your Pig's loyalty or faithfulness to you on such an adventure, we're sorry to say you have concerns beyond the scope of this book. Pig weekends are mostly just Pigs doing stupid Pig stuff.

When Pigs are all together again in a pen, they tend to let loose, connect and release the pent up frustrations of trying to live in today's world. They talk shit. They laugh with and at each other. They give each other advice. They eat and drink whatever the hell they want with no consideration for health or wellbeing. They can burp, fart, snort, grunt — secure in the knowledge that the other Pigs are okay with it and that they're just being the Pig that they are.

TIP: *Do not pry into the trip and what happened. This annoys the Pig. The weekend therapy will be more successful if you let your Pig communicate about it on his terms, when he's ready (please note this may be never).*

We tell you the following not to hurt your feelings but just as an FYI: on Pig weekends they almost never talk about you! While relationships are likely of paramount importance to you and you might spend a fair amount of time with your friends talking about them, the opposite is true for the Pig. It just hardly ever comes up. That's not to say you are not important to your Pig, but when Pigs get together they just don't often talk about their relationships...sorry ladies but that's the truth.

Special Events

For special events, including weddings, funerals, other extended family events, charitable functions, theater outings, and clubbing, your Pig can rise to the occasion when he wants to. It is key, however, that he knows three simple things. Be very clear about these so that your Pig *gets it*:

- **What to wear**

Pigs like to be comfortable, both physically and socially. Though his default might be shorts and a tee-shirt, if the other Pigs are wearing Dockers® and sports coats, or dinner jackets and dancing pumps, your Pig wants to fit in, so paint the scene for him and make a few suggestions (not demands). Most Pigs will appreciate a little helpful advice on proper dress for the occasion.

- **When to be ready**

Being on time for things is easy and important for most Pigs. Give him a specific time to be ready or when to pick you up, and then be appreciative and punctual yourself. Of course most Pigs understand that it takes women a bit longer to dress and be ready. We understand that and are generally accepting of it unless it runs to more than half an hour.

- **Where to show up**

This is especially important if your Pig lives in his own pen or if you are meeting him somewhere. Be as specific as possible and even provide a written address or directions if your Pig is challenged in this area. Make sure that you welcome him when he arrives. Nothing is better than being met at the door of a restaurant by a smiling, well dressed woman who makes it known to all that her Pig has arrived.

Fighting With a Pig

Never wrestle with a Pig. You're both going to get dirty, but the difference is, the Pig likes it. It's important to understand what fighting and arguing looks like to your Pig before you get into it. Depending on the situation you might not be able to tell if he thinks you're just rolling in the mud or if he perceives it as a real threat.

Men are competitive creatures by nature. They will compete at any game, sport or activity with any one at any time. Hell, they'll even race a train to the next crossing if they think it would be fun, worth winning and there is an audience. Reminds me of an old red neck joke, a Red Necks last words, "Hey y'all, watch this!" That Red Neck was a ~~man~~ Pig...you can bet on it!

We'll compete for who can swim across the river, who can eat the most hot dogs, who can drink the most beer, who can fart the loudest, who can jump across the chasm without falling to our death. Competition is what makes us who and what we are. This is a good thing when properly applied. It's what makes some of us better providers than others since the job market (as seen by men) is just another competitive sport.

So what's all this got to do with arguing with a Pig? Well, men see a good argument like they see any other competition. Some one wins, some one loses and there is a bunch of fun along the way. Sounds like a football game or a hockey match. That is exactly the way a man sees a good argument. If there is an audience to the contest, even better. The thing to keep in mind is that a man will do ANYTHING to win a competition. He'll sustain incredible punishment (physical or emotional) so long as he comes out the winner. A man knows the pain of the battle will fade. The scars will heal. But, the pain of losing will stay with a man forever. Most of us still know who won and lost any major game in the last 20 years, so don't think we ever forget who won or lost an argument over the remote control. Winning becomes the only objective. When our honor is at stake and thoughts of our legacy are in the backs of our minds, death is even favored over losing. Most men would prefer, in order of preference: Winning. Death. Losing. In that order. Not healthy? Not smart? Not logical? Welcome to the mind of the Pig.

Losing is not an option. Win at any cost is his mantra. Why, you ask, should you engage any creature who thinks this way? How can you possibly come out ahead (also called winning) unless you are prepared to be as ruthless, cruel and brutal as your Pig?

So, are you still asking what's that got to do with arguing and fighting with a Pig? Winning at any cost is the only way a Pig knows to play. It almost doesn't matter what the argument is about. Or who is right or wrong. It only matters that he does not lose. If you understand this, you are armed with one of the most important tools in the management of your Pig.

So, how to prepare for the argument? First, make sure it's an argument worth having. Will it actually resolve anything or is it just a fun contest to see which of you is the winner?

Let's say you do decide to fight and that by some miracle you actually do "win." (By the way this is not terribly hard since Pigs are not the brightest creatures, especially when they're competing). So there you are, you have won. Using wit, wisdom, intelligence and cunning you have managed to outrun his corner backs, outsmart his quarterback, and leave his defensive line in shambles. A quick look at the scoreboard confirms that You Have WON and Won BIG. Congratulations....Time to celebrate the win.

Not so fast. To the Pig this is just the first of a three game series. You can bet that at some level he's already planning a strategy for game 2 and it won't be long before you are back in the mud wrestling for your life. We may shake the hand of the winner and have a beer while smiling and laughing, but inside we are already planning where to bury the body after the next battle.

Make sure that the outcome of your argument leaves your Pigs ego intact and if at all possible make the argument a discussion that ends with the two of you arriving at a joint conclusion as opposed to your making your point and "winning."

Make Wrongs

A make wrong is an attack on your Pig about what he said or did. Usually make wrongs are there to make *you* right. A make wrong will piss off your Pig even if he did make a mistake. Make sure you know what you're trying to get out of it or if you're just trying to piss the Pig off. Ask yourself what you're trying to achieve and catch yourself before you do it. Make wrongs do not further the conversation and are usually an attack on the Pig. They will respond accordingly.

Things Pigs usually dislike

- Buying feminine hygiene products
- Dancing
- Going to the mall
- Did we mention dancing?

What you should have learned in this chapter

- Lists are good. Good lists are great. Give your list to him and let him do his thing. Reward him.
- Your Pig needs Pig friends and Pig-only excursions. Support him in these endeavors and be grateful.
- Set your Pig up for success in polite company by giving him clear instructions on what to wear, when to be ready, and when to show up.
- How to fight
- Making wrong
- Things Pigs hate

5

Communication

"A man never tells you anything until you contradict him."
~ George Bernard Shaw

IT'S POSSIBLE, THOUGH NOT always easy to communicate with a Pig. In fact, Pigs are communicating almost constantly, they just don't talk very much and it's usually in the form of a grunt, groan or burp. Now you might try and teach your Pig to talk, however, teaching a Pig to talk is frustrating and it really annoys the Pig. Besides you often lose the essence of the Pig Type that attracted you in the first place.

It's easy to learn a few simple communication tools that will help you understand the simple communication style of your Pig and make use of his existing skills.

A Pig's personal communication techniques will be closely related to his Pig Type and affected by his State. Much of what we'll say in this section is general in nature and meant to be a guide to Pig communication — a primer. Over time you'll develop an understanding of your particular Pig's vocabulary and style.

When Pigs are out together at sporting events or Pig weekends, occassionally the conversation will touch on their relationships, usually the ones with women. Pigs usually know they're not very adept at managing their relationships, they will communicate with other Pigs to learn two important things. First, are their communication expectations realistic? Second, do the other Pigs have similar issues or other desires?

We've spoken with many Pigs about this and engaged in some rough-and-ready field surveying, asking "What do you want from your woman?" We've compiled their remarks into a few strong themes.

The biggest complaint is that women never ask for what they want or they ask indirectly. The Pig often doesn't understand that he's being questioned or he's confused about what he's being asked. He'll get frustrated because he wants to jump in and help but doesn't have a clue about what that might be. Ideally a conversation with your Pig would begin as an unadorned request, and then, if required, embellished with details, story, color and emotion.

We are simple creatures and have simple needs. Don't make them more complex because you think they're simple or suspect there is a deeper meaning. Basically, your Pig wants to know you hear, appreciate, trust and truly value him as a uniquely lovable and flawed Pig.

What Pigs Want

Let me know you love me and that you are happy

- Tell me you love me, show me you love me, and just love me
- Remind me what characteristics you really love about me.
- Leave me little notes now and then in strange places to let me know you're thinking of me.
- Tell me often when you are happy with me and our relationship — this makes me feel like a success and gives me confidence.
- Don't make me wrong for being who I am. Let me know you appreciate me for the qualities and behaviors I have. Give me freedom to "show up" how I want to — not how you think I should.

Make me your king; I will make you my queen

- Say and do things for me that make me feel like your man.
- Let me treat you as my lady and my Queen.
- Let me know I can take care of you.
- Make me your hero and make me feel there is no other guy that can do it quite like I do.

Trust me

- Don't show me how to do something. Trust that I can do it myself.
- Trust me with important decisions.
- When I ask you something simple, don't always ask why.
- Work with me so I can give you what you need and want.
- It's okay to ask for help, but please be specific about the request before telling the story.
- When you open up and let me in, this shows me you trust me.

Talk with me, not to me.

- Look me in the eye when you speak to me and always be truthful. This shows me you are sincere and respectful of both of us.
- Present things in an open way, requesting honest feedback.
- Pointing out how important things are for the kids, for you, or all of us as a family puts me in touch with a higher purpose than just doing something because you are beautiful & sexy.

- If you ask a question please consider my answer.
- Ask me anything and don't think I can read your mind.
- Don't assume you know what I am thinking or feeling,. Ask me in a safe environment and I will be happy to tell you.

Make our communication a priority

- Let's set time aside to just have a conversation without all the noise of life around us.
- Ask me for time to talk about something you are frustrated with instead of keeping it to yourself. This shows me you want our relationship to be strong and open.
- Don't bring drama to our relationship in order to create communication. Tell me how you feel without guilt or games.
- If you want to talk I will listen. When I am done listening, accept it with grace and understanding.
- Quiet times together are as special as those when we're communicating.

Tips for communicating with Pigs

The following are our tips for how to achieve successful communication with your Pig. Communication will flow easier and you'll receive a positive response from your Pig if you use the following tips.

Communication Tip #1:

Listen — but not in the usual way you do with women.

Maybe you're thinking; "My Piggy doesn't talk to me." While your Pig may not "talk" to you much, you can bet he's nonetheless communicating. A dog doesn't talk, and yet we understand all of his needs, his likes, and his dislikes. A scratch at the door means "I have to pee, let me out." When he puts his head in your lap, he wants to be petted. And when he brings you his empty food bowl, he's telling you he's hungry. Dogs do a pretty good job of communicating their needs and their love for us without actually talking.

It's the same with Pigs. You'll need to learn a bit of "Pig speak" and become an acute observer of Piggy body language, but once you do you'll be able to communicate very effectively with your Pig and he'll be able to communicate better with you.

It's sort of like taking your dog to obedience school and teaching him a few simple commands. You're both learning. He's learning how to be rewarded by responding consistently and in particular ways to certain sounds and gestures. You're learning how to make him want to do things he would do anyway, as well as things he would never do if left to himself,. You learn to communicate with him effectively, and he learns to respond and be rewarded.

When the system works, everyone is happy. When it doesn't, nobody is. When it doesn't work, take the opportunity to observe his non-verbal language, interpret it and tailor your next approach accordingly. Don't ever make the mistake of assuming that since he's not talking, he's not broadcasting on other frequencies. Learn to tune in.

Communication Tip #2:

Watch what your Pig does, not what he says.

Pigs communicate primarily through their actions and mostly without words. A Pig's actions almost never lie, whereas he'll lie with his words. It's not because he intends to be deceitful, but because he often doesn't know what's true or not. Remember, he does not naturally use his higher cognitive skills to evaluate his feelings and emotions. He just acts. These thoughtless actions are most often true and authentic indications of what's going on well below his conscious awareness.

Some classic reasons a Pig will lie to you (and himself): to get laid; to avoid or put an end to an argument; to make you think he's strong; to avoid telling you what he knows you don't want to hear.

Yes, with his words he'll lie, lie, lie...but he'll behave consistently with his true self. Learn to understand your Pig's actions and you have a true and faithful understanding of what is *really* going on with him, regardless of what he says.

Let's look at an example. You have a first date with a new Pig and things go well. You have a really wonderful time and think that maybe this is someone who could be worth getting to know. Then he doesn't call. Days go by and you don't hear from him. Finally you call and he says, "Gee, really good to hear from you. I've been really busy at work and my car is in the shop. Very sorry."

You naturally understand his being busy. But the *truth* is in his actions: he didn't call. It's safe to assume he didn't think the date went as well as you did and his actions are doing the talking. Believe me, if he shared your feelings about how well the first date went, he would have called no matter how busy he was or how many other things are going on in his life. You could have moved, changed your name and had plastic surgery, and he still would have found you if he had wanted to.

Look at the *actions* and ignore all the words (well, except a few which we'll cover later).

Communication Tip #3:

Find a safe, simple Pig environment.

Pigs need to feel comfortable and safe to be able to open up. Discover what that safe pen looks like so you can go there when you want him to communicate with you. It could be at a sports bar, in a particular room, walking hand in hand in the park. Don't try to guess this one—just ask, listen and summarize to be sure you are getting it. Once you think you understand, do trial runs with easy subjects. When your Pig knows he has a place to go with you where he's safe, he'll reveal his world of feelings and thoughts.

Hint: open ended questions and deep listening works best.

The more important the discussion, the more important it becomes to move to a safe Pig pen environment *with no distractions.* A sports bar during the playoffs of his favorite team is not the place to have a serious discussion about where your relationship is going or how he feels about your new hair cut. The context and timing is way off and will irritate the Pig.

Communication Tip #4:

Never ask a Pig what he's thinking.

Unless he's already and very obviously fully engaged, it leaves him with only two choices: lie or start a fight. Remember, just as you would not seriously expect an intelligent response from your dog or cat to that same question, you should never expect anything more from your Pig.

Chances are very good that whatever he's thinking at any moment has something to do with breasts (yours or someone else's), a bimbo, a ball, a fast car, the latest movie review, or an explosive charge. This is why Pigs develop a standard "Oh, nothing, honey" sort of reply. This is a survival response, since by the time Pigs reach the age of about twenty, they have learned that answering this question honestly will usually put them in hot water. Fast.

For example, let's say you are in the final stages of the conversation with your Pig deciding whether to paint the guest bath Mojave Sunset or Sierra Dawn. So far, you have already eliminated 50 or 60 colors in the hours-long discussion, which has stretched from your visit to the paint store after lunch to dinner at Leroy's Wood Pit BBQ. Now back at the house, you've settled in to make the final choice. Her internal dialogue: "Once this decision is made I can move on to that all-important choice of accent color for the adjoining guest bedroom, and then those wonderful throw pillows for the bed from either Linens 'n Things® or Bed Bath and Beyond®. If it's Bed Bath and Beyond, then I can go during lunch hour tomorrow as my boss will be on the road to Denver and Janice can cover the phones for an extra few minutes since I took her shift last week while she was having lunch with that wonderful new guy she met at the concert last month. Of course, I'll have to take the car instead of walking because I'll need the trunk. Why Janice is so crazy about this cowboy is a mystery. Maybe she's just on the rebound from that trucker she was dating for awhile. What a loser...but nice buns."

Then you notice that your Piggy is staring at the color cards and looking kind of pensive and thoughtful. You think maybe he has an insight into the Sierra Dawn/ Mojave Sunset decision and you ask "So, what are you thinking?" It's really beyond comprehension why, in this moment, you actually expect an intelligent thoughtful and on-topic response from your Pig. Why not just ask your cat?

His honest reply—if he were dumb enough to tell you—probably would be one of the following:

"That waitress at dinner sure had a nice rack."

"That hard body who helped us with the samples at the paint store didn't have a brain but must be one wild bronco…YEEE HAAAA!"

"What in the world was he thinking, going long on third and 5 in the forth quarter? They need to trade that idiot."

"I'm sure that the 69 Cobra® could wipe a Corvette® Z06, no matter what Bob says."

"If I packed 5…no 10 lbs of high explosive C4 in the shitter, could I blow this F&*!$* bathroom to Portland regardless of the color?"

Since your Pig knows that none of these answers will be anywhere near your idea of the "right" one and will only reveal that he's not following the color thing, he simply applies the universal "Nothing dear." If he's a little more advanced, remembers your topic, and is a little horny, he may suggest that maybe the Sierra Dawn is closer to the color of your eyes on the beach during that first sunset in Hawaii on your honeymoon…

Hey, this is a Pig you're talking to! Give it up! He doesn't care about the color of the guest bathroom. If it was up to him, he would tape a Playmate centerfold to the back of the door and stock the open floor space with Hot Rod® and Sports Illustrated® magazines. Just like his bathroom when you met him, remember?

So, unless you are fully prepared to hear an answer similar to the ones above, give up asking Pigs what they're thinking. The answer is: not much and certainly nothing of real value.

Communication Tip #5:

Timing is Everything.

You've heard the saying "there is a time and season for everything." When Pigs are hungry, tired, stressed, angry, anxious, resentful or threatened they're really not receptive or thinking clearly. These are not the times to bring up anything important.

When your Pig does say something to you, immediately compare it to his State. If necessary, deal with his State first, then talk. A Tired, hungry Pig is not able to see much beyond his need to kick back and be fed, so feed him and leave him alone for awhile. Then, when he's Happy or even Horny, you have the keys to his motivation. "Yes" is so much easier to get to when his energy level is up and he feels capable and confident,. Look for times that are favorable to discuss your issues and desires.

Plan *how* you are going to communicate based on what response you want from your Pig. If you want your way, be open to receiving what you'll suggest he give you. If you want to understand what's going on in his mind, create a safe place for him to tell you. If you are already angry and want to fight, corner him and get loud. Your choice.

Communication Tip #6:

Forget "Win-Win" Arguments.

For a Pig, a "win-win" argument is when you lose twice. No one wins an argument with a Pig. You might feel like you've won but you'll have lost in the long run because it's in a Pig's nature to fight or flee when confronted. If you argue to win every time with your Pig, he'll lose interest and shut down all communication. If he cannot see a mutually satisfying solution to the situation, he'll not feel that a successful conclusion has been reached and he'll remain frustrated.

Ask yourself whether your intention is to prove your Pig wrong, to communicate and share your feelings, or to discuss what a mutual solution looks like. Protracted arguments make Pigs stake out their turf and defend it. The more you try to make him wrong, the harder he'll resist. Just because a Pig stops arguing with you doesn't mean you've won. He may have simply stopped talking.

The purpose of an argument is to achieve understanding. You might have to settle for being understood or agreeing to disagree rather than getting your Pig to give in. Agreeing is a choice between two people. An excellent rule of thumb for going into any argument is to have three possible solutions ready to roll and then be open to your Pig's ideas.

Communication Tip #7:

End the conversation.

Don't leave an open end to a conversation with a Pig, especially if it can become a sore point that's brought up over and over again down the road. Complete the conversation and move on, otherwise the Pig will feel overwhelmed when trying to recall where you left off and what is still up for resolution. Make sure you and your Pig have finished the topic or be sure to table it for a time when it's better for the two of you.

Communication Tip #8:

K.I.S.S. (Keep It Simple, Sweetie)

Pigs do not multi-task. They can, under duress, but it's a sad thing to witness. A Pig is at his best when he can focus on one thing at a time. Don't ramble and switch and connect topics — this only overwhelms and frustrates him. Pick one topic or issue, work it through, get it resolved, then take a breath. This gives him a chance to save that file where he can easily access it again. If you let topics merge together or wander off, your Pig won't see your logic and will stop listening to you. He'll assume that what you're talking about is not the real issue and will have his guard up, waiting until you say something he can latch onto. Your best plan when talking to any Pig is: Stay on track, communicate inoffensively, and be willing to resolve and complete.

Don't talk to your Pig while he's doing something unrelated to what you're saying. Introducing new material into his airwaves when he's focused on something only degrades his attention level to the detriment of everything around him. It may confuse him and he'll certainly be frustrated. Wait until his attention is ready for a new focal point, then introduce your topic. *Hint:* open with just 25 words and only one topic or concept.

Communication Tip #9:

Ask your Pig how to communicate with him.

Sometimes you have to stop guessing and just outright ask what the best way to communicate with your Pig is. His answer might be something simple (by email), or this question will confuse him. If nothing else, it will catch him off-guard and you'll have his undivided attention, if for only a moment. Whether you like his suggestions or not, thank him and give it a try. Determine whether it works for you in practice, and then improvise to satisfy you both.

Communication Tip #10:

Ask open-ended questions

Yes or no are rarely adequate choices for answers to real questions and a Pig may feel you are trying to trap him with an either-or choice. Make your Pig feel understood and valued by asking thoughtful questions. Be sincere and inquisitive. Listen to what he says and take it at face value. Spend less time trying to make him understand you and your needs and more time making him feel heard and understood. When you do this, his natural reaction is to come around and eventually inquire about your needs. If your Pig knows you care about him he's more likely to make sincere efforts to be clear in his communication

Communication Tip #11:

Flattery Will Get You Everywhere. (Especially if it's based on reality, even loosely.)

Pigs have nine different kinds of egos and like to be acknowledged for what they feel are their strengths. Complimenting your Pig on his strengths and rewarding him for using them well will enable him to shine and feel special when he's around you. The fact that you recognize his favorite attributes about himself will make him appreciate you for being nice and special enough to tell him how wonderful he's. Just don't overdo it! If your Pig thinks you are insincere in your flattery, he'll be hurt. When complimenting your Pig, notice his reaction. He should square his shoulders, smile that cute smile at you and perhaps blush a bit and let out a little "Aw, shucks, ma'am" kind of thing. Showing a little humility is a good thing.

Communication Tip #12:

Use your Femininity to Activate his Masculinity. Fair is fair.

Pigs are typically visual animals. While we've a keen sense of smell and are profoundly affected by perfumes and pheromones, our conscious experience with women is that we are visually stimulated. Each Pig has certain characteristics that he likes best though he may only be aware of the most obvious ones: T & A, legs, smile, and hair. He'll be glad to tell you what draws his eye first and you may be surprised by his preferences. Go ahead and ask him what he finds attractive about you. He knows very well what that is and if he's thinking at all he may take the opportunity to wax poetic over your beauty. Listen well, accept the compliment with grace, and store the information for later use.

Once you have identified his favorite features, you can highlight them in your dress and manner. When your Pig sees you, his woman, as a vision of his feminine beloved, it brings out his masculinity. He'll feel proud to be seen with you and act from the protector mode of his ego because he knows other Pigs will notice you as well. How could they not?

Communication Tip #13:

Rule Of Holes — When you're in one, stop digging!

If you make a mistake with your Pig admit your error, cry if you have to, and move on. Don't try to explain your way out as your Pig doesn't care and it could cause him to get defensive and feel he needs to prove his point about how you blew it. Pigs have an inert bullshit meter that goes off when they realize the woman talking to him is trying to sell her way out of her error. A discussion around the issue shouldn't be tied to the admission of guilt at that particular time. If you must, take it up again later when your Pig is in a better State for interaction.

Communication Tip #14:

Ask for what you really want.

Subtle does not work with Pigs. Don't even try to convince yourself it does. Don't waste your time being coy or pussyfooting around. Just say it, whatever it's, as succinctly as you can, choosing your words and tone to match the reaction you want. Don't make a statement when you really want to ask a question or take an action. Don't have an opinion about everything. It doesn't further the conversation to get into a debate because you want to express your opinion.

A special communication tip:

Ya Buts

The meaning of the word "but" is "behold the underlying truth" Ya Buts tell a Pig you're not listening to him. It sends off a secret message that you want to get into an argument. This denial of Pig validation pisses off the Pig and will cause frustration in the Pig.

Hint: If you hear yourself say "ya but" stop, listen and validate. If the Pig does a "ya but" to you, another approach needs to be taken with the Pig.

What you should have learned in this chapter

- Pigs communicate differently then women — learn to recognize the signs
- Pigs need to feel unique and special — find ways to acknowledge that you know them
- Be in sync with the different communications techniques — think simply and direct
- Learn the communication style that works for your Pig

6

The Matrix

"This is your last chance. After this, there is no turning back. You take the blue pill – the story ends, you wake up in your bed and believe whatever you want to believe. You take the red pill – you stay in Wonderland and I show you how deep the rabbit-hole goes.

~ Morpheus from the movie *The Matrix.* © 1999 Warner Bros. Entertainment Inc.

Demystifying Pigs

Forget the old saying that "a little knowledge is a dangerous thing." When it comes to Pigs, a little knowledge is *all* you need. Many experts would argue that the more knowledge you possess, the more you can appreciate the individuality and nuances of that person.

A predicament chart, when used correctly, is a useful guide to help a person answer the questions "What happens if I encounter a Pig in a certain State and do X to them". It also answers "When should I do different things to get different reactions?". The chart is subjective generalizations that assume healthy normal conditions. Additional pieces of information are also included to give you an idea of the **quality of the outcome.**

A predicament chart should indicate that given a steady State you can provide effective communication to your Pig before reacting. Typically we all react based on our beliefs, thoughts, past history or experiences. We do not process everything in a rational logical fashion. By looking at the chart and knowing some key tips and techniques for communicating with Pigs, you can stage a much more proactive approach to insure you communicate effectively with the Pig.

To Begin

Choose a "State" from the top of the predicament chart. Next, select the action or behavior you would like to display. Move your fingers down and across from your selections to see your predicted outcome.

For Example:

Your Pig is noticeably "Happy" and you decide to "Laugh with me" in conversation. Put your finger on Happy and follow it down until you find laugh with me. The square indicates Happy/Horny/Excited (this is a good thing).

The KnowyourPig! © Predicament Matrix

State →

Action ↓	Happy	Hungry	Hurried	Horny	Angry	Tired
Engage Me	H	?	?	?	A	?
Feed Me	H	H	?	?	?	H
Avoid Me	A	?	H	?	H	H
Piss Me Off	A	A	A	A	A	A
Communicate with me	H	?	?	?	?	?
Offer Me Sex	H	?	?	H	?	H
Mother Me	?	A	?	A	A	?
Ignore Me	?	?	H	?	H	H
Laugh at Me	?	A	?	?	A	A
Laugh with Me	H	?	?	H	?	H
Smother Me	?	?	A	A	A	?
Mock Me	A	A	A	?	A	A
Disrespect my State	?	?	A	?	A	A

Key:
- Angry — Bad, angry, confronting.
- Moody — 50/50 and can go either way.
- Happy — Happy/Horny/Excited.

Mothering vs. Smothering

There is a fine line between mothering and smothering. Most Pigs are happy to be left alone and do not require much maintenance once their environment is set up. Sometimes it's nice to be mothered — like when a Pig has had a crappy day at the office or he just needs a breather from life. Mothering is something you do when you're in a medium gray (H) zone on the predicament chart in a communicating mood. Sometimes it's 15 minutes once a month; sometimes it's once a week. It all depends on the Pig. Just watch out — if a Pig wants to be mothered all the time you might have a mama's boy on your hands — you need to decide if that works for you. On the other side, if you find yourself wanting to mother *all* the time, perhaps you need to stop looking for a Pig and seek out a dog, cat or plant. Just a thought.

What you should have learned in this chapter

- Pigs follow simple patterns and modes in their respective States
- Always ask yourself what State the Pig you're dealing with might be in.
- If unsure, ASK! It's better to ask than assume you know.
- Try making your own predicament table for each key Pig in your life.

7

The Pig Types

> *"...all I want is for one guy to prove to me that they aren't all the same..."*
> ~ Kaitlin Harris
>
> *"There's someone out there for everyone — even if you need a pickaxe, a compass, and night goggles to find them."*
> ~ Steve Martin

BELOW ARE OUR interpretations and descriptions of each of the nine Pig Types. No one type is better or worse than the other types and should be given consideration as to what type(s) work for your personality. The Pig Types are:

Type One:	The Excellence Pig
Type Two:	The Charitable Pig
Type Three:	The Acrobat Pig
Type Four:	The Sentimental Pig
Type Five:	The Watcher Pig
Type Six:	The Unbeliever Pig
Type Seven:	The Gourmet Pig
Type Eight:	The Guard Pig
Type Nine:	The Diplomat Pig

Type One Excellence Pig

Type One Pigs are conscientious and ethical, with a strong, persistent, even Pig-headed sense of right and wrong. They're likely to launch into sudden and puzzling crusades to make changes to the pen, but underneath this bluster they're afraid of making a mistake. Excellence Pigs are well-organized, orderly, and fastidious (even prone to bathing themselves and cleaning their bathroom). Sometimes you just want to roll them in the slop to wipe that look off their snouts. They're usually loners in the pen because the other Pigs get tired of the constant fixes going on around them. Not surprisingly, they have problems with resentment and impatience. At their best they're wise, discerning, realistic, and noble. At worst they're insufferable Pigs.

Type Two Charitable Pig

The Charitable Pig is the caring, interpersonal type, often considered by women to be rare and highly desirable. In close proximity, however, he's all too familiar. And we mean *all* too familiar. Although they're well-meaning, you sometimes have to ask a Type Two Pigs to back off. This hurts their feelings and they'll retreat to a corner of the pen and snuffle inconsolably. Charitable Pigs are friendly and generous but can also sink into being sentimental, flattering, and self-sacrificing. They typically have problems with possessiveness and acknowledging their own needs, preferring instead to lurk at the end of the trough with a hollow look in their little eyes, hoping for sympathy. This touchy-feely Pig can irritate other Pigs with their outwardly feminine traits. Women usually have lots of these Pigs as friends and feel understood by them. At their best, Type Two Pigs are unselfish and altruistic with seemingly unconditional love for others. At their worst they're simpering and codependent.

Type Three Acrobat Pig

The Acrobat Pig looks good with you on his arm — and he knows it. Type Three Pigs are adaptable and success-oriented, self-assured and charming. If you want one that brings home the bacon (wrapped around slices of smoked salmon with a sliver of scallion), this is your Pig. Ambitious and energetic, they can also be image- and status-conscious to a laughable degree. Just don't laugh at them. Ever. Other Pigs get jealous because they're compulsively competent, handsome and quick to attract women. Type Three Pigs have a rotating stable of Type Three Pig buddies with whom they get together to sculpt their pecks, advise each other about women, and hone their wine critique vocabularies. Type Three Pigs often have problems with workaholism and competitiveness, raising the probability of an early demise. At their best they're self-accepting, authentic, role models who inspire others. At worst, they're peacocks who spend a lot of money on dinner.

Type Four Sentimental Pig

The Sentimental Pig is a favorite of frustrated artists and well-heeled Type Three wives. They're introspective and romantic, often to the point of moody narcissism, though they can segue seamlessly into disarming emotional honesty and self-pity. Their highly-developed creativity can preclude any real comprehension of reality, something they find disdainful and exempt from by virtue of their inner angst. This dramatic and often public wallowing can drive their fellow Pigs to the other side of the pen and others to drink. At their best they're inspired, startling and able to renew and transform themselves. At worst, they're useless.

Type Five Watcher Pig

The Watcher Pig is fascinating, insightful and curious. He has a powerful brain and is not afraid to use it. These Pigs intimidate by just being in a room. At cocktail parties they delight in cornering other Pigs in abstract or scientifically obscure discussions, reducing them to cinders before the admiring eyes of Type Three Pigs and their cohorts. Type Five Pigs are likely to have bizarre hobbies they consider more important than their relationships, wardrobes, and vocations which may be spotty at best. These Pigs will occasionally withdraw into lengthy periods of solitude, during which they require necessary assistance with basic hygiene and nutrition. At their best, Type Five Pigs are visionaries who acknowledge no box from which to think out of. At worst, they're hopeless nerds.

Type Six Unbeliever Pig

This Unbeliever Pig wants to be on your team and you want him there. In fact, you want several Type Six Pigs on your team, but not more than 30%. Once the Unbeliever Pig is with the program, especially if he's passionate about you, he'll be there 125% as long he feels respected, useful and able. Like Dobermans, Type Six Pigs show up best when they're doing a task they can execute well and receive praise for. Left idle, they will assign themselves tasks not necessarily in line with what everybody else had in mind. They will, however, pursue these tasks with stubborn vigor until completed. Other Pigs put up with their eagerness because the Type Six Pig will carry his own load and the loads of others as well. The Unbeliever Pig requires special handling when stress levels rise. They're good planners and excellent at enlisting others in their projects but their underlying self doubt will make them suspicious and defiant if they feel their authority is being challenged. Type Six Pigs will send for take out. At their best, Six Pigs are reliable, courageous champions. At worst they're Dobermans.

Type Seven Gourmet Pig

This Gourmet Pig is great fun to have in your life, but over the long haul can be exhausting to less exuberant types. When you get his attention, the Seven Pig can be counted upon for an unusual perspective on just about anything. This is derived from his many and diverse interests and accomplishments. The Type Seven Pig is always in the process of constructing a pattern for his observed and theoretical universe — a bright, beautiful, hopeful pattern, indeed. He can get quite carried away by his fascination with life, leading to impulsive behavior, irresponsible novelty-seeking and excess in many pleasures including food, addictive substances, travel, sex, and beautiful objects. The Seven Pig can actually get quite manic, something other Pigs may find exciting at first; but when the crash comes, the Type Seven Pig becomes alarmingly dark. Gourmet Pigs live for their personal freedom and happiness and like to maintain a high level of excitement to avoid pain. At best, the Seven Pig is purposeful, joyous and grateful for the simple wonder of boundless life. At worst, he's shallow, pointless and self destructive.

Type Eight Guard Pig

The Guard Pig is unmistakable: he's the King of the Pen (or believes he should be). In domestic situations he can have no doubt of his dominance, whatever the reality. From his throne of self-confidence, the Eight Pig is protective, honorable and takes satisfaction in his mastery over the real world. Financial independence, physical safety and control of his life are his priorities and he's willing to take heroic risks to assure these conditions. This Pig will not stop short of confrontation and intimidation when he deems it necessary to correct and maintain his social or professional order. A highly successful or delusional Type Eight Pig can be a real pain in the hams and other Pigs in his pen may band together and rebel, leaving the Eight Pig stripped of his identity. He has great difficulty being emotionally vulnerable as he sees this as a weakness. To achieve intimacy with a Guard Pig, his partner must establish safety through trust and respect, never, ever violating it. At their best, Type Eight Pigs are heroic, honorable and inspiring. At worst they're dangerous.

Type Nine Diplomat Pig

The Diplomat Pig is the perfect foil for the Type Eight Pig in friendship and work. His easy-going optimism has a calming influence, sometimes to the point of being hypnotic to other Pigs. These Pigs are always asking, "Can't we all just get along in the pen?" driving other Pigs completely nuts, especially Threes, Fours and Sixes. In stressful times, the Nine Pig's natural presence, desire for peace, and talent for communicating make him an excellent mediator or synthesizer. He's able to see both sides because he has no strong opinion about either, only in maintaining the peace. His self-possession and contentment make a Type Nine very easy to live with, sometimes too easy. They do not mind having a fire lit under them so long as it's free of conflict. Type Nine Pigs are capable of profound relationships and startlingly deep communication. At best, they're intensely alive and connected to themselves and others. At worst, they're genuinely indifferent slugs.

What you should have learned in this chapter

- There are nine Types of Pigs, each of which has its own particular trait pattern present in differing degrees according to individual tendencies.
- Every Pig Type has characteristics worth admiring. And some to despise.
- It's useful to be able to anticipate Pig behaviors, as they occur in the sets described.
- You'll recognize several of your friends among the Types, and should be starting to get a picture of which Pig Type you would be, if you were a Pig.

8

Putting it all together

"It requires wisdom to understand wisdom: the music is nothing if the audience is deaf".
~ Walter Lippmann

FROM THIS POINT ON we're going to pull it all together and give you a starting point for Knowing Your Pig! The idea here is to arm you with the right tools and wisdom to approach your Pig situation with a new perspective. Just like learning a new trade, these new tools will seem foreign at first. Like the first time you drove a car — it was little weird and didn't make a lot of sense, but eventually you got it. No problem.

So where do you start?

The map below will gives an overview of the steps you should take to begin to understand the Pigs in your life.

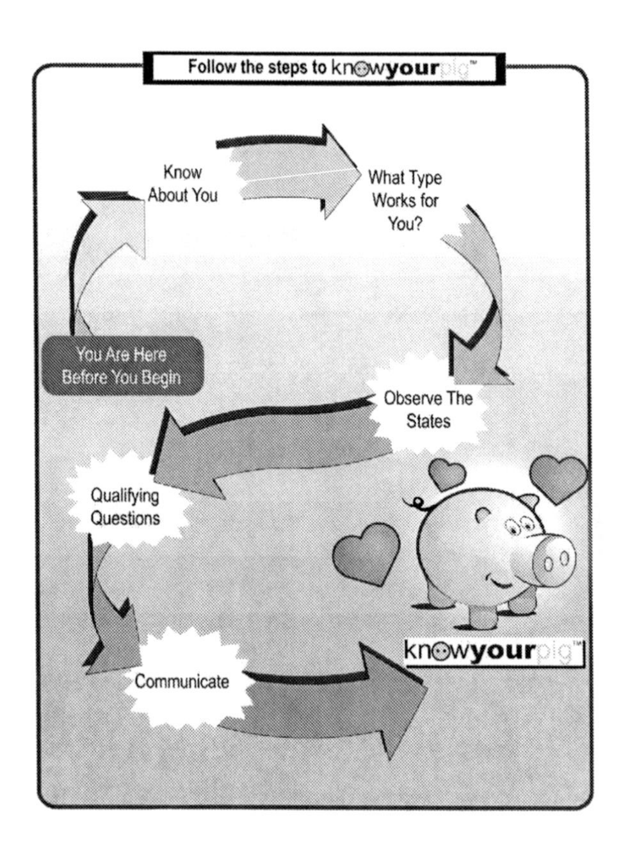

You Are Here

Before you engage Pigs, you have to know who *you* are. Everyone has visited a mall wanting to find a store quickly but getting lost in the process. You should always start out by going to the directory and looking for the "you are here" dot on the map. Understand where you're coming from first — Do you know where you are in the relationship? Do you know what really works or what the other person is all about? Put yourself in a third party observer mode and see if you can tell what you really know. Are you experienced with Pigs or just starting out? There is an old Chinese saying, "If you're a hammer, everything looks like a nail". What tools do you have in your kit of tricks that work? What hasn't worked in the past? Developing an awareness before you start using a new approach will help you know when you're on track and when you're off.

However, presuming that you have decided to take the plunge and select a pig of your own to manage and love then just like deciding to get a puppy, there are a few things you should take along the way to insure your success and the pig's happiness.

Admit to yourself that you want a pig. Become comfortable with the idea of having a pig knowing full well the challenge you are taking on. No matter how carefully you screen the man, in the end he will be a pig and you will be faced with the inevitable challenges of owning, caring for and managing your own special little oinker.

What Type Works for You?

Your understanding of Pigs — simplify your approach by reading the descriptions and getting a gut feel for what Types work well for you. Look into your past, current and desired relationships to see which ones fit your criteria. Which ones worked well in your life 'til now? Can you guess the Types of Pigs you interact with every day? Try and learn the nuances of the Pig Types and be sure to question and observe their behaviors to see if they exhibit the Type you selected.

Be prepared to admit that you gave up too soon on Pigs and need to qualify them better. It's said that people give up to soon when they're close to success. Learn to ask better questions and listen to what is said instead of what you want to hear. It's hard to listen to your gut and trust what you're hearing or seeing. As we mentioned above, actions speak louder then words. When qualifying, listen to what you say when asking questions of Pigs. You'll learn a lot based on the way you ask questions. It's easy for the brain to trick you into believing that you said something a certain way when it was actually quite different.

Do you notice physical, auditory or literal attributes in Pigs? What is your style of receiving information? This might bias you towards certain Pigs over other ones.

Decide which of the nine types of pigs you are best suited to work with. Each will have its own unique challenges and rewards so there is no "right" answer on this one. However, you will discover that your personal style and life style will be more compatible with some of the types than others.

Observe the States

Observe the States and how you engage with them. Test yourself when you encounter a Pig at work, home or out in society looking for what State he's in and how he communicates in that State. How do you feel when you experience the different States? How long does it take for you to pick which State they're in? A bar makes it easy to default a Pigs State as horny. But can you spot the ones that are not? What States are they in? Notice reactions to your requests during the different States. This one is good to reflect on and notice behaviors. Just remember, it isn't always about you and you might be taking something personally it really isn't.

This might be the hardest step of them all; Become comfortable with the simplicity of the pig. They're just not that complex as we hope you come to realize by now. Understand the six states, and how to recognize them in the pigs with who you deal. This includes respecting the states and how to utilize them.

Qualifying Questions

Ask qualifying questions and listen for key words. Qualifying questions are open-ended questions that let someone communicate where they're coming from. They get people to talk and ramble, providing lots of information. It also lets you learn about their thoughts, feelings and the general direction of the conversation. Listen and record what they say. Do you ask questions looking for a specific answer? Are you afraid to ask the hard questions of your Pig or yourself? A Silver Bullet question to ask yourself before engaging a Pig is "What do I know that I am pretending not to know"?

Communicate

Try communicating based on the approaches outlined in previous chapters. Try it first on safe and simple topics so you can notice the answer and how it affects you. You'll be surprised at the outcome. Simpler is better. Short, sweet and to the point. In the worst case, you can have a full discussion with a Pig about Pig communication.

Déjà vu!!! Whoa....we've entered the "Twilight Zone" by watching and observing our Pig communicate about communication!... Try it out... you'll be amazed. The Pig might be defensive at first as once you start talking on a level normally reserved for other Pigs. Don't let this dissuade you — the Pig will feel comfortable once he realizes it's with good intent. If your Pig stops too soon without giving you enough information, simply say "tell me more".

So have fun. *Seriously,* have fun! Life is too short and stressful to miss out on fun in a relationship! It's been said that for every troubling situation in your relationship, you need five times the number of fun situations to balance it out. Humor is the common glue of conversation and in opening doors. Help us help you Know Your Pig!

We Would Like To Hear From You

If you have a funny story from using the Knowyourpig book, please let us know. We also welcome your thoughts and comments.

Send us your feedback at *info@knowyourpig.com*.

Suggested Reading List

The Female Brain

Written by **Louann Brizendine, M.D.**

ISBN: 978-0-7679-2009-4 (0-7679-2009-0)

Men Are from Mars, Women Are from Venus

Men Are from Mars, Women Are from Venus: A Practical Guide for Improving Communication and Getting What You Want in Your Relationships (Hardcover) by **John Gray**

ISBN: 006016848X

The Proper Care and Feeding of Husbands

The Proper Care and Feeding of Husbands (Hardcover) by **Laura Schlessinger** (Author)

ISBN: 0060520612

He's Just Not That Into You

He's Just Not That Into You: The No-Excuses Truth to Understanding Guys (Hardcover) by **Greg Behrendt, Liz Tuccillo**

ISBN: 068987474X

The Essential Enneagram

The Essential Enneagram: The Definitive Personality Test and Self-Discovery Guide (Paperback) by **David N. Daniels** (Author), **Virginia A. Price**

ISBN: 068987474X

About the Authors

Michael Coogan

Born and raised in Denver, Colorado, Michael has traveled the world and experienced people from all walks of life. His humorous views and comments of the human condition draw attention to the view that we all have simple truths and feeling we all want to experience. He has spoken to large groups as well as couples both domestically and internationally. He also coaches salespeople in processes and presentation skills.

William Burton

A Pig by birth and a student of the human condition for more than 50 years, William is a frequent speaker to small groups of men and couples where he shares his unique and often hilarious views of what it means to be a man in today's complex world. He's managed by his current wife who uses many of the technologies and techniques discussed in the book to keep him both happy and out of trouble. He has three grown children and is currently the President of an aviation business in the Sacramento area of California.

FREE Newsletter

The authors invite you to join their newsletter mailing list. The newsletter will provide great stories, tips, book reviews, special offers, advance notices of new books, and commentary in the same fun tone as the book. You can join the newsletter mailing list directly by going to *knowyourpig@aweber.com* (This is the service that manages our mailing lists). You can also go our site and sign up there, *www.knowyourpig.com*. And if you sign up now, we'll send you a free gift as a thank you!

Professional Speakers

Both Michael Coogan and Bill Burton have International speaking experience. If you wish to contact the authors to arrange for a professional speaking engagement, they can be reached at *speaker@knowyourpig.com*.

Stories and Testimonials Needed

We are always looking for good story contributions of inspiration, hope, fun, and overcoming relationship and communication challenges. We welcome your stories and testimonials for Know Your Pig. Please send an email to *support@knowyourpig.com*. We WILL acknowledge each and every submission!

The End!

Global Focus
2710 Thomes Ave.
Suite 370
Cheyenne, WY 82001

info@knowyourpig.com
www.knowyourpig.com

Printed in the United States
205207BV00008B/3/A

9 780978 817619